ARTISTRY

IN

WOOD

New Ireland Wooden Male Figure, (Melanesia, South Pacific). Height 54½". Much primitive art in wood has been destroyed by the inroads of colonialism and natural decay; what remains is highly valued in today's art market. This carved figure sold for $13,000.00 at auction at Parke-Bernet Galleries in New York, where an even smaller carving, a 33½" figure from the Cameroons set a record at $29,-000.00.

ARTISTRY
IN
WOOD

IDEAS, HISTORY, TOOLS, TECHNIQUES: CARVING, SCULPTURE, ASSEMBLAGE, WOODCUTS, etc.

by M. VINCENT HAYES

DESIGNED BY
PAT E. HAYES

DRAKE PUBLISHERS, INC.   NEW YORK

Acknowledgment

I wish to express my appreciation to the consultants, galleries, museums and libraries whose help made the writing of this book a real pleasure.

Most of all, I want to thank the artists, past and present, who acquired the skill to make their diverse visions tangible and accessible to us through the use of a few tools and pieces of wood.

Introduction

Wood is one of the most accessible of the art mediums. Throughout the centuries it has stirred the imagination and invited the tools of artists and craftsmen. Some of the world's finest artworks have been produced in wood.

Today, the challenge of wood remains as great as it ever was — for the experienced artist, for the student seeking a medium in which to express his ideas, for the inveterate "whittler," and for anyone who likes to take a natural material in hand and speculate what he could make of it if . . .

A practical book, *Artistry in Wood* aims to help you across the bridge that divides dreaming from doing. It combines instruction with ideas, and illustrates the great tradition of artistry in wood. It tries to show the endless variety of objects that is possible in wood and to remove any preconceptions about wood being limited to a few styles and techniques. You may not like all the objects illustrated in this book, but you won't come away with the impression that wood is a limited medium.

While the traditional may be exciting and inspiring, the not-so-traditional may be even more so. And the beginning artist is encouraged to try many different approaches, to experiment with different techniques, and to attempt to express his ideas in a variety of styles.

Copying is part of the traditional training of artists. So is continuous observation. Examine sculpture and woodcuts and constructions and reliefs at first hand whenever you have an opportunity. And use the illustrations to make comparisons, to note the different ways the artists achieved their effects.

You're not required to buy a roomful of expensive tools, nor do you need to serve a long, painstaking apprenticeship before beginning to work in wood. But there are some requirements: the desire to visualize what a piece of wood could be; the willingness to try, and not reach perfection, and then to try again. To really observe the shapes and forms you encounter every day. And above all, to want to explore, experiment; to want to think by touching, and make contact without words.

Use the illustrations in this book as ideas and bridges to your own creations. Visit some of the museums listed in this book and examine their artworks in wood. Consider creativity as a continuous learning and doing process. Let your attitude toward your work be that of Renoir. When in his 80's and an acclaimed artist he told a friend, "I am beginning to learn something about painting."

Coquille Nuage, by Jean Arp. 1933. Wood decoupage, 22¼″ x 15½″ x 1⅛″. Courtesy Sidney Janis Gallery.

Methethy as Mature Man, Egyptian, VI Dynasty, about 2340 B.C. Courtesy, Brooklyn Museum. Charles Edwin Wilbur Fund. Wood covered with gesso. The frontal pose and the attempt to realize a close likeness of the person represented are characteristic of Egyptian sculpture of this period.

History

Woodcarving has always been one of the most intimate and comprehensible of the arts. Wherever it was practiced — in ancient Egypt, medieval Europe, primitive Africa, among the American Indians — it drew for inspiration on the day-to-day life of everyman: his concern for family and household; his delight in anecdote and fable; his apprehension and wonder at what lies beyond.

The early history of woodcarving is still being written, as archaeologists continue to retrieve objects from the past. And despite their efforts, large gaps will remain to pique our curiosity. For although wood was among the first materials used by man to fashion his tools and utensils, it is by nature perishable.

Fortunately, we are able to reach back into the past some 5000 years to the tombs of ancient Egypt. From these treasure houses of the dead, archaeologists have brought to light superbly crafted items of furniture, small, finely carved toilet articles, ornamented walking sticks, models of homes and shops, and carved figures of the buried nobles and warriors. The contrast between polished and carved sur-

Virgin and Child, artist unknown, South German, 15th Century. Courtesy Parke-Bernet Galleries, New York. The gothic cathedrals abounded with fine sculpture. Along the aisles and in the many interior chapels the statues of Virgin and Child, scenes from the Passion and representations of saints, followed one after the other. While the subjects were exalted, the artist took his models from his family and the townspeople who lived in the shadow of the great churches. In this 37″ high polychromed statue, the woodcarver never permits the religious theme to obscure the simple humanity of a very real mother and child who lived some 500 years ago.

Virgin and Child, Romanesque, 13th century. Oak. 31″ high. Courtesy Wadsworth Atheneum, Hartford. It is interesting to imagine how this piece would look today if the artist had used walnut instead of oak.

faces, the careful carving of face and body, the restrained use of decoration, all testify to the high degree of skill and sophistication reached by these unknown artists in wood.

In Europe, the earliest remaining evidence of artistry in wood dates from the Romanesque period (500 to 1150 A.D.), when carvings began to adorn the abbey churches. During the Gothic period (1150 to 1550 A.D.), the rise of the great cathedrals offered the woodcarver the widest range for his skills in the carving of choir stalls, canopies, arm rests, and the massive oak chests which served as chair, table, bed and storage space.

By the 15th century, woodcarving had become a fluid and expressive medium in the hands of expert and highly re-garded craftsmen. Churchmen, nobles and merchants now demanded increasingly elaborate carving, complex pat-terns and tracery with which to embellish the richly furnished churches and palaces; and the artists and their apprentices gladly complied. Figures of popular folklore and legend, Reynard the Fox and the Washerwoman, ornamented the massive furniture , while classical motifs appeared on pilasters, cornices and lintels.

With the decline in power of the religious and popular symbols which had infused the art during the Gothic period, woodcarving lost much of its basic human appeal. Tech-nical mastery continued to grow. But unsustained by a con-trolling belief or idea, it led to artificiality and exhibitionism.

In the Far East too woodcarving proceeded from the religious to the secular. By the 16th century, the artists turned from the temples, where their carvings played a basic role, to the shrines of the wealthy merchants, where conspicuous decoration enhanced the status of the owner.

Particularly in China did the carved ceilings and elaborately decorative tracings on furniture serve as an expected mark of distinction in the palaces of nobles and the mansions of successful merchants. The Japanese, on the other hand, excelled in the production of netsuke, small, figuratively designed buttons on which the wearers strung their pouches for money and medicine.

Graceful and imaginative woodcarving was executed in England during the 18th century, and in colonial America until well into the 19th century, the artist in wood exercised his skills on furniture, weathervanes, hitching posts, and figureheads for ships' prows.

Leonardo da Vinci had argued with Michelangelo that painting was superior to sculpture, and little was produced by the art academy between the close of the Renaissance and the opening of the 20th century to refute him. Some fine work continued to be executed by the cabinetmakers to provide decorative objects for a dwindling aristocracy and a rising middle class. But even this limited demand for the woodcarver's art diminished with the growing availability of factory-produced furniture and household items. Fascinated with the machine, the consumer no longer considered "made by hand" a mark of distinction.

Statuette, Chinese, Chou Dynasty, 5th to 4th Century B.C., lacquered wood, 24¾" high. Courtesy, Wadsworth Atheneum, Hartford. This statuette, made in the Yangtze Valley as a tomb figure, is one of the earliest examples of Chinese wood sculpture. The carver made no attempt at realism, obtaining his effects with planes and a formalized rendering of the head.

Zuni War God, American Indian, New Mexico. Courtesy of Galerie Kamer, New York. The highly stylized approach of the American Indian to carving is evident in this portrait of a war god. Note how the cylindrical mass of a pole has been retained to define the outer dimensions, while the carved planes and angles are kept to a minimum. Observe also how the passage of time and the natural decay of the wood contribute to the powerful effect.

Carved Wood Statue of *Tamonten*, Chinese, Kamakura Period. 46½″ high. Photo courtesy of Parke-Bernet Galleries. The standing king with furled eyebrows and closed mouth wears armor with skirt, and supports in his upraised right hand a trident. His left hand holds a small pagoda.

Saints, German, 18th century. Wood with silver gilt, 34½" high. Courtesy of Parke-Bernet Galleries.

Carved Wood Chess Set, artist unknown. Courtesy Parke-Bernet Galleries. Probably carved around 1737 in Augsburg, Germany, this chess set brought $8,-000.00 at auction. Compare the realistic figures, from 2¾" high to 3¼" high, with the abstract chess set illustrated in this book.

The one exception to this trend lay outside the academic tradition entirely, in the realm of folk or naive art. Throughout the ages, untutored woodcarvers had served the everydays needs of their people for utensils, weapons, objects which would both serve a material function and carry a weight of symbolic meaning. That many of these objects are of a rare beauty and distinction is evident from the illustrations of American Indian and African carvings in this book.

Although the American Indian drew many of his motifs from his day-to-day experience of nature, the art he produced was highly stylized, intended to serve the ends of religion and ritual. He manipulated abstract designs into multitudinous patterns which, no matter how complex, made a statement understood by every member of the tribe.

Equestrian Figure, Yoruba Tribe, Nigeria. Wood.
Photo courtesy of Galerie Kamer, New York.

When the Indian carved into the long poles the decorative designs and symbols that functioned as totems, these identifying insignia of family and tribe were presented, not as naturalistic depictions of bird and animal, but as crow, bear, beaver and wolf shaped according to the rules of a convention more rigid than those imposed by any academy. Yet despite the limitations within which he worked, perhaps even drawing strength from the knowledge that, although his carving vocabulary held but few words, those few were the sacred words of his people, the Indian woodcarver achieved in his totem poles, ceremonial masks and household items a vigor and power of expression which may be unequaled on this continent.

Like the Indian, the primitive African woodcarver conceived of his art in religious terms. He invested each carving with a particular symbolic meaning, designed each statuette of god and goddess, each life-size ceremonial mask, to perform a definite function in a system of beliefs shared by the artist and his public.

To copy nature was not his responsibility; rather it was to make nature comprehensible and emotionally manageable. With remarkable invention and dexterity, he used distortion and emphasis to give symbolic meaning to individual parts of the human and animal form, to take full advantage of the artistic potentialities of the wood, and to combine symbol and function in the same object. Sometimes elaborately embellished with incised carvings, sometimes awesome in its simplicity, the work of the African artist was to become a major force in the development of modern art.

Objets Celestes, by Jean Arp. 1961. 30" x 30". Courtesy Sidney Janis Gallery, New York. To create an object with its own plastic identity that would not be an imitation of something else became one of the ambitions of the artists who broke with the realist tradition preceding World War I. Throughout his career, German artist Jean Arp continued to refine this ambition, carving faultless reliefs and sculptures that are awesome in their simplicity. Note how in this wood relief both two and three dimensional effects are achieved by superimposing carved painted forms one over the other on a wood panel, which is in turn mounted on another background, and the whole enclosed with the plainest of frames.

Mask, Fang Tribe, Gabon. Wood. Courtesy Galerie Kamer, Inc.

Two Children are Threatened by a Nightingale, by
Max Ernst. 1924. Oil painting on wood with wood
construction. 18″ x 13″. Collection, The Museum of
Modern Art, New York.

Women and Dog, By Marisol. 1964. Wood, plaster, liquitex and miscellaneous items. 72″ x 82″ x 16″ deep. Collection of Whitney Museum of American Art, New York. Gift of the Friends of the Whitney Museum of American Art. Marisol frequently incorporates her own features in her art constructions. The "miscellaneous items" in the Museum's description include a real pocketbook, dog chain and collar, dog's head, the bow on the little girl's head. This artist is an excellent draftsman, painter, carver — and carpenter, with exceptional skill and imagination.

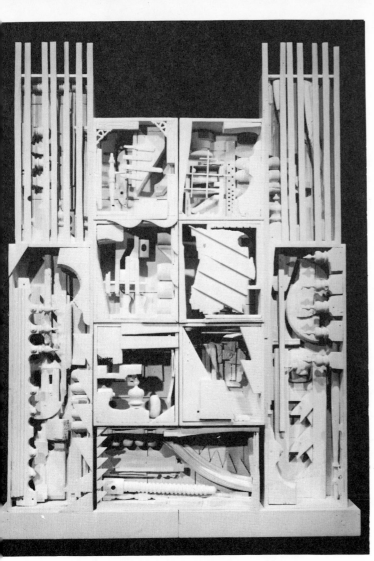

Dawn's Wedding Chapel II. Louise Nevelson. Painted wood. 116″ high, 83″ wide, 10½″ deep. Collection of the Whitney Museum of American Art. Gift of the Howard and Jean Lipman Foundation, Inc.

Pyramid, by Carl Andre. Courtesy of Dwan Gallery, New York. Joining pieces of wood together can yield more than carpentry. In this construction, the simplest of wood strips have been assembled into a form 68⅞″ high to create an impression of dignity and strength which amply justifies the title. Mathematically precise planning and disciplined use of the wood grain of each piece are basic to the total effect.

Not until about 1900 did the trained artist again begin to work in wood with imagination and a sense of creative purpose. A major reason for the resurgence of the wood medium at that time was the breaking down of the barriers that had hitherto separated the several arts. Whereas only a few 19th century artists tried their hands at both painting and sculpture (Degas and Gauguin are notable exceptions), in the 20th century Munch, Feininger, Picasso, Matisse, Ernst and Giacometti were representative of many who worked fluently in more than one medium.

In denying that valid boundaries existed between painting and sculpture, these modernists let into the world of artistry in wood an invigorating breath of fresh air. The vocabulary and techniques of Expressionism, Cubism and Surrealism, which had revolutionized painting, had an equally shattering impact on the woodcut and wood sculpture. Indeed, a new and broader definition had now to be given to the latter term as it came to include assemblage, construction, collage and any wood object, alone or in combination with other materials, that functioned aesthetically.

The discoveries of primitive African art by archaeologists in the late 19th and early 20th centuries — discoveries which exerted a primary influence on the development of Cubism in painting — did much to dictate the choice of wood as a working medium by the modernists, and shaped their conception of forms and planes as stylized, non-representational entities. It was a short but significant step which then carried sculptors Constantine Brancusi and Jean Arp from this simplification and purification of forms to total abstraction, where only the essence or "spirit" which lay hidden in the wood would be revealed. Fascinated by the innate possibilities of their material, Brancusi and Arp, along with Henry Moore, dispensed with working from the model and reasserted the primacy of direct carving. Following World War II, however, Moore was to return to the human form as the major theme for his work.

Also abstract, but concerned with the manipulation of space rather than the revelation of the form within the wood, was the work of the Constructivists. With strips of wood, wire and other materials they enclosed space in rarefied constructions of great delicacy, designed according to geometric principles.

The continuing strength of the abstract tradition is evident in the work of many of the young artists in wood working and exhibiting in the '70's. Assemblage and construction abound, some airy and seemingly floating in space, others, made of heavy beams, so massive in scale they seem like some prehistoric monument dropped onto a city square or into an open field to startle and trouble the passers-by. Created with power tools in workshops according to the artist's plans, chemically preserved against the elements, they combine the traditional values of wood with the technology of the day.

A vigorous realism also flourishes. It draws its inspiration from the contemporary scene, upon which it comments critically and satirically, and uninhibitedly uses every woodworking technique available. Carving, painting, photog-

26

raphy, collage combine to produce a new excitement, proving that artistry in wood remains very much alive.

Woodcuts

The oldest of the graphic processes is the woodcut. It was practiced in China over a thousand years ago as a substitute means of producing inexpensive religious paintings. The technique soon spread to Japan, where there arose a succession of master woodcut artists who for the first time conceived their designs in terms of the wood block and thus raised the woodcut to the level of a primary art technique.

During the 15th century, the woodcut became very popular in Europe, first as a means of decorating playing cards, and then as a pictorial medium. Printed in quantity, woodcuts on religious and mythological themes were frequently grouped together to form picture books. When captions were carved in the block below the illustration, the pattern for making the first type for printing was established.

Between 1492 and 1526, Dürer, the earliest European master to work with the woodcut, made drawings expressly for this medium which were then cut into the block by craftsmen-woodcarvers. This separation of function — the

Marcus Curtius, by Lucas Cranach the Elder (1472-1553). Woodcut, 13⅛″ x 9⅜″. Courtesy of the Kennedy Galleries.

artist executing the drawing, the craftsman doing the carving, and the printer doing the printing — characterized the woodcut process until modern times.

The woodcut continued in popularity until the 19th century, when the dominance it shared with the lithograph as an illustrative medium was threatened by the invention of the daguerreotype. Early in this century, however, under the stimulus of color woodcuts produced in China and Japan, modern artists returned to this traditional medium with enthusiasm. Matisse, Picasso, Munch, Feininger set new levels of excellence for this oldest of the relief processes.

Shepherd Corydon from Eclogues of Virgil, by Aristide Maillol. 1912-14. Woodcut, 3$^{15}\!/_{16}$" v 4⅛". Collection, The Museum of Modern Art, New York. Henry Church Fund.

Hockende, Erich Heckel. 1914. Woodcut. Courtesy, Martin Gordon Gallery. The woodcut became an important means of expression to a group of artists formed in Dresden, Germany, in 1905, and called The Bridge, to which Heckel belonged. They sought to attain the same combination of mysticism and realism in the graphic arts which they found in the sculpture of the Gothic period, and to some extent they even imitated the life style of the Gothic craftsmen, living and working together, drawing on a communal supply of money, tools and materials, and helping each other to produce their woodcut prints. But they also absorbed into their work the influences of primitive and oriental art.

Wood

The artist in wood is never bored by his materials, for no two pieces of wood are exactly alike. Each will challenge, delight and sometimes exasperate you with its display of personality traits and idiosyncrasies.

Handle wood with the respect and understanding that a live medium deserves, and it will graciously yield its wealth of patterns, designs and surfaces, imparting to your work an enduring vitality and sensuousness. But if you try to impose your will on wood through sheer force, brushing aside its waywardness and individuality, it will splinter, split and stubbornly resist your most determined efforts with knife and chisel.

Practically any wood can be carved, assembled or painted to produce a work of art. But some understanding of the characteristics and varieties of wood will make it easier to select the most congenial for your work and then to incorporate its particular structure and grain pattern into your design to the best advantage.

To grasp the fascination of wood as an art medium, spend a few minutes studying the cross-cut of a log. At the very center is the pith, the point from which the young tree grew in thickness. At the extreme outer surface is a protective coating of bark.

Surrounding the pith and reaching outward to the cambium, a microscopically thin layer between the bark and the wood where the new growth takes place, is a series of concentric annual rings, the number depending on the age of the tree. Cutting across the annual rings and extending outward from the pith to the bark like the spokes of a wheel, are many thin lines, called medullary rays. These cell structures may be invisible to the naked eye in some woods, but contribute strong design elements in beech and oak.

You will note that most of the cross-cut, specifically that section nearest the center which is known as the heartwood, is comparatively dark and stable in color. In this section of the tree the cells have ceased to grow, and its fibres and vessels have become clogged. Dead, hard and durable, it is the timber most favored by sculptors.

The sapwood, on the other hand, which is nearest the bark and is marked off by the outer, or most recent, annual rings, is still in the process of growth, and its living cells are therefore subject to disease. Lengthy seasoning and impregnation with wood preservatives are advisable before committing your design to sapwood.

It is the direction of the fibers in the wood, referred to as

Cross section of white ash log showing the pith in the direct center, the dark area of surrounding heartwood, and the lighter area of sapwood extending out to the bark. The concentric circles extending through the entire cross section are the annual rings which mark the history of the tree's growth. The heartwood, or darker section, is the most valuable to the artist in wood, as it is composed of dead cells which are less open to attack from insects and fungi while in the softwood the live sap is still rising.

the grain, which gives to your particular block or panel its individuality and personality. Sometimes forming a relatively simple pattern, and at other times an extremely complicated one, this compact mass of wood cells differ widely in various kinds of wood. Generally this fibrous structure extends vertically for the length of the tree, which is why it is easier to split a log up and down (working with the grain) than to attack it horizontally.

The unpredictability of wood occasionally raises a few problems. But don't discard a piece of wood just because you discover a knot or burl in it. A knot is simply the root of a branch which became embedded in the trunk of the tree and blocked the path of the fibers, causing them to detour. As your skills develop, you may delight in weaving this "fault" into the design. Similarly, a burl is not a disaster. While difficult to work with, this outgrowth which appears on the trunks of some trees compensates for its contrariness in handling by offering an abundance of striking patterns.

What you do want to avoid is unseasoned wood, which has a heavy moisture content and is thus subject to warping, shrinkage and attack by fungi. Nor should you attempt the difficult and sometimes dangerous seasoning process yourself. It's too easy to buy at your lumber yard seasoned boards and logs which have been commercially dried in kilns or in the open air.

When ordering wood commercially, you will immediately be confronted with a choice between what the botanists term "hardwoods" and "softwoods." The "hardwoods" are derived from broadleafed trees like the oak, ash and maple, and generally are not as easy to work as the "softwoods" because of their density and complex cell structure. But the extra effort they require is more than balanced by their qualities of durability, smooth finish and tactile appeal.

"Softwoods" are derived from coniferous trees, such as balsam, cedar and pine. They are more porous than "hardwoods," have a simpler cell structure, with most cells aligned up and down the tree, and are subject to shrinkage and warping.

This terminology should be handled with caution. Not all "hardwoods" are hard in the sense of being difficult to work with, and not all "softwoods" are easy. The best insurance against confusion is a visit to your lumber dealer (on one of his slow days if possible), and a leisurely examination of the different woods. Try to come away with as many scraps and samples as possible, so you can study the woods at home and experiment by working with them.

Like most artists, you will find the search for woods a continuing challenge. Some look for timbers and other elements from old buildings being torn down, as well as old pieces of furniture. Certainly these "found" materials possess the advantage of proven durability, and their varying shapes, sizes and colors may suggest unusual designs and images to your mind. Indeed, the "found" object, only slightly modified by the artist and placed in an art context, has led to a new category of art work.

Sailor, by Emanuel Romano. Woodcut (birch), 9" x 12½". Note the contrast of black on white for the upper half and the white on black of the lower. It would be interesting to see the block from which this print was made. This artist uses many kinds of woods, even kitchen cutting boards, for his woodcuts.

The Horse, by Alexander Calder. 1928. Walnut, 15½" x 34¾". Collection, The Museum of Modern Art, New York. Acquired through the Lillie P. Bliss Bequest. Carving and construction combine in Calder's wittily stylized horse. Observe the way the sculptor has incorporated the pattern of the wood grain in the design.

For the beginner, it is advisable to work up gradually to the truly challenging woods, such as velvet black *lignum vitae*, which is extremely hard, or the rich-toned ebonies, and to start instead with the woods which are comparatively soft and possess a more or less straight grain.

Here are a few good "starter" woods:

Basswood, which has an even texture, is light in weight, and lends itself easily to your first carving efforts. Creamy brown in color.

Butternut, with a more interesting, albeit coarse, grain pattern, is easy to work and has a cocoa to chestnut brown color.

Cedar is straight-grained, with a pink to red color, and is also easy to work. But be sure you enjoy its powerful odor.

Fir, another easy wood, creamy yellow to reddish in tone, is one of the softest woods — indeed, it is so soft that all but the sharpest tools will merely bruise or dent it instead of cutting. It has strong, well-defined lines and is creamy white in color. A good practice wood.

White pine is equally encouraging to the beginner, and has the added advantage of carving neatly and sharply, and glues well in lamination.

Redwood is somewhat harder but still a relatively undemanding wood. It is recommended for outdoor sculpture where the ability to carve in broad, bold outlines and resistance to weather are considerations. Straight grained, cherry to brownish red, with excellent texture.

Among the harder woods you can then advance to are:

Mahogany, in various tones of dark brown and red; Honduras and Philippine mahogany are the least exacting and the lightest in color; West African mahogany is also recommended. Most of the mahoganies yield rich effects after sandpapering and polishing.

Oak, one of the traditional woodworking materials, is also one of the most versatile, suitable for indoor or outdoor work. With age, its brownish-yellow tones tend to deepen. Excellent grain. But you need sharp tools, whose visible marks will contribute handsomely to the design. More appropriate for bold conceptions than for delicacy of detail.

Walnut is another hard wood which polishes and works well. It exhibits a close, straight grain with interesting figuration. This pattern is most pronounced in the English, Italian and French types and less conspicuous in American or black walnut, although the latter compensates with its deeper tones.

As you select your woods, keep in mind that the close-grained woods are usually the most suitable for work you intend to be rich in detail and highly polished, and the coarse-grained woods more appropriate for your broadly defined designs, where the rougher finish contributes to the visual impact.

Not a natural wood but widely used by contemporary artists is plywood, which is made up of thin layers of wood laminated together with glue. Plywood may be purchased in varying degrees of thickness and grade.

Whatever wood you select, expect its unique characteristics to play a decisive role in determining the overall effect of the work. Wood stubbornly insists on maintaining its individuality, nor would the artist have it otherwise. For it is the dynamic interaction of artist and material which gives the finished work its vitality and enduring interest.

Frequently, you will begin with one image in mind, only to modify it as the spirit of the wood manifests itself in the emerging colors, patterns, forms.

However, when you do want to execute a specific design, be sure to select a "cooperative" wood. Examine the rhythm and varying grain patterns, determine to what extent they will contribute to the realization of your goal. Don't, for example, try to convey an impression of delicacy and grace with a wood that boldly vaunts its strength.

Mother and Child, by E. Glicenstein. 1938. Mahogany, 31" x 14". Collection of Hugo Dreyfuss.

Kneeling Virgin, Flemish or Lombard School, 15th century. Lindenwood, 47" high. Courtesy, Wadsworth Atheneum, Hartford. Neither worms nor wear nor weather could destroy the breathtaking purity of this carving.

Short Glossary of Wood Terms

Annual growth ring — The growth layer put on in a single growth year

Bark — Outer layer of a tree, comprising the inner bark, or thin living inner part, and the outer

Bending, steam — The process of forming curved wood members by steaming or boiling the wood and bending it to a form

Cambium — The one-cell-thick layer of tissue between the bark and the wood that repeatedly subdivides to form new wood and bark cells

Cell — a general term for the minute units of wood structure, including wood fibers, vessels, members and other elements of diverse structure and function

Decay — The decomposition of wood substance by fungi

Dressed size — The dimensions of lumber after shrinking from the green dimensions and being surfaced by a planing machine to usually 3/8 or 1/2 inch less than the nominal or rough size. For example, a 2- by 4-inch stud actually measures 1-5/9 by 3-5/8 inches under American lumber standards for softwood lumber

Fiber, wood — A comparatively long (one twenty-fifth or less to one-third inch), narrow, tapering wood cell closed at both ends

Figure — The pattern produced in a wood surface by annual growth rings, rays, knots, deviations from regular grain, and irregular coloration

Grade — The designation of quality of a manufactured piece of wood or of logs

Grain — The direction, size, arrangement, appearance or quality of the elements in wood. To have a specific meaning the term must be qualifid:

Close-grained wood — Wood with narrow, inconspicuous annual rings

Coarse-grained wood — Wood with wide, conspicuous annual rings in which there is considerable difference between springwood and summerwood. The term is sometimes used to designate wood with large pores, such as oak, ash, chestnut and walnut, but in this sense the term "coarse textured" is often preferred

Cross-grained wood — Wood in which the fibers deviate from a line parallel to the sides of the piece

Straight-grained wood — Wood in which the fibers run parallel to the axis of a piece

Green — Freshly sawed lumber or lumber that has received no intentional drying; unseasoned. The term does not apply to lumber that may have become completely wet through waterlogging

Hardwoods — Generally the botanical group of trees that have broad leaves in contrast to the conifers or softwoods. The term has no reference to the actual hardness of the wood

Heartwood — The wood extending from the pith to the sapwood, the cells of which no longer participate in the life processes of the tree. Heartwood may be infiltrated with gums, resins and other materials that usually make it darker and more decay resistant than sapwood

Knot — That portion of a branch or limb which has been surrounded by subsequent growth of the wood of the trunk or other portion of the tree. As a knot appears on the sawed surface, it is merely a section of the entire knot, its shape depending upon the direction of the cut

Moisture content of wood — The amount of water contained in the wood. Usually expressed as a percentage of the weight of the ovendry wood

Nominal size — As applied to timber or lumber, the rough-sawed commercial size by which it is known and sold on the market

Old growth — Timber growing in or harvested from a mature, naturally established forest

Ovendry wood — Wood dried to constant weight in an oven at temperatures above that of boiling water

Pith — The small, soft core occurring in the structural center of a tree trunk, branch, twig or log

Plywood — An assembly made of layers (plies) of veneer, or of veneer in combination with a lumber core, joined with an adhesive. The grain of adjoining plies is usually laid at right angles, and almost always an odd number of plies are used to obtain balanced construction

Porous woods — Another name for hardwoods, which frequently have vessels or pores large enough to be seen readily without magnification

Preservative — Any substance that is effective, for a reasonable length of time, in preventing the development and action of wood-rotting fungi, borers of various kinds and harmful insects that deteriorate wood

Radial — Coincident with a radius from the axis of the tree or log to the circumference. A radial section is a lengthwise section in a plane that extends from pith to bark

Sapwood — The living wood of pale color near the outside of the log. Under most conditions the sapwood is more susceptible to decay than heartwood

Seasoning — Removing moisture from green wood in order to improve its serviceability

Softwoods — Generally, the botanical group of trees that bear cones and in most cases have needlelike or scalelike leaves; also the wood produced by such trees. The term has no reference to the actual hardness of the wood

Springwood — The portion of the annual growth ring that is formed during the early part of the season's growth. In most softwoods and ring-porous hardwoods, it is less dense and weaker mechanically than summerwood

Stain — A discoloration in wood that may be caused by such diverse agencies as micro-organisms, metal or chemicals. The term also applies to materials used to color wood

Summerwood — The portion of the annual growth ring that is formed after the springwood formation has ceased. In most softwoods and in ring-porous hardwoods, it is denser and stronger mechanically than springwood

Texture — A term used interchangeably with grain. Sometimes used to combine the concepts of density and degree of contrast between springwood and summerwood

Veneer — A thin layer or sheet of wood cut on a veneer machine

Vessels — Wood cells of comparatively large diameter than have open ends and are set one above the other so as to form continuous tubes. The openings of the vessels on the surface of a piece of wood are usually referred to as pores

Weathering — The mechanical or chemical disintegration and discoloration of the surface of wood that is caused by exposure to light, the action of dust and sands carried by winds, and the alternate shrinking and swelling of the surface fibers with the continual variation in moisture content brought by changes in the weather. Weathering does not include decay

Wood substance — The solid material of which wood is composed. It usually refers to the extractive-free solid substance of which the cell walls are composed, but this is not always true. There is no wide variation in chemical composition or specific gravity between the wood substance of various species; the characteristic differences of species are largely due to differences in infiltrated materials and variations in relative amounts of cell walls and cell cavities

Workability — The degree of ease and smoothness of cut obtained with hand or machine tools

The complete glossary from which the above has been adapted is contained in Agricultural Handbook No. 101 produced by the Forest Service of the United States Department of Agriculture. This booklet, *Wood: Colors and Kinds* also contains detailed descriptions and properties of many American woods.

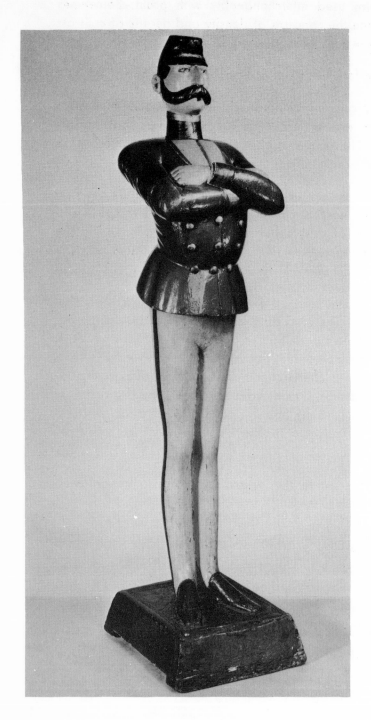

Captain Jinks of the Horse Marines, American, 19th century, artist unknown. 75″ high. Wood, painted. Collection of the Newark Museum, gift of Herbert E. Ehlers. Intended as a satirical portrait of the Emperor Franz Joseph by its carver, a German sculptor and caricaturist who came to this country after the revolution of 1848, this 75″ high carving stood at Newark's four corners, Broad and Market Streets, for half a century.

The Work Place

Where the artist works is usually a matter of circumstances. Probably more masterpieces have been created under make-shift conditions than in dream studios. Today, some of the most vigorous creative work in wood takes place in walk-up lofts in run-down sections of the cities, in store fronts devoid of natural light, and in sheds and barns which have been converted into woodworking "studios" by the determination and muscle of the artist alone. The important thing is to make the best of whatever space you have, arranging workbench and tools and materials for maximum convenience.

Sometimes this means juggling several values. You may be forced to choose between good lighting and a minimum of traffic, for example. Since you can do something about the lighting with electricity, but it's difficult to reroute human beings, particularly your own family, settle for the area where you can work with minimum interference.

You need a sturdy, secure workbench, with a top surface at least two inches thick and large enough to accommodate the wood you intend to carve as well as a comfortable layout of the tools. The surface level should be high enough to permit you to work while standing without bending over. Be sure the surface overlaps the framework sufficiently to accommodate a vise and clamps for securing the wood for your project.

Before beginning, spread the tools out before you on the workbench in orderly fashion. When not in use, they can be clipped to a wall-mounted pegboard within arm's reach of the workbench — or stored in individual cloth pockets and placed in a box or drawer. Tools turn dull or get mangled when allowed to rub and bump against each other.

Aim for the arrangement of the work area that will best serve in your particular circumstances. Figure in all factors before you finalize your set-up: room to move about, so you can approach the project from different sides; light directed on the work area (and not on you); accessible tools. It's a good idea to stay flexible for a while until you can test the arrangement under actual working conditions.

The hollowed-out cylindrical mass of wood on which Hostetler works already suggests the finished form. Observe, in the standing figure, how the tool marks are retained over the entire surface to enhance the rough-hewn character of the work. Photo Courtesy of the Sculpture Center.

Japanese Woodcarver at Work, date unknown. Courtesy Rowland's Antiques, Buckingham, Bucks County, Pa. It is interesting to see the tools this artist used. Note, too, the surface texture and the simple grace of the drape.

Tools

One of the delights of artistry in wood is that there are so few equipment roadblocks to getting started. You can make your first carving with an ordinary jackknife, your first sculpture with a chisel, a few gouges, a rasp and a mallet, and your first construction with ordinary household carpentry tools. It's not the extent of your investment in "tooling up" that is important, but your resourcefulness in working with what you have.

Work at first with a minimum of tools, then build up your inventory as the need arises. And before purchasing, check your tool chest to avoid duplication and unnecessary expense.

Keep in mind that you do not need all of the tools listed below to turn out creditable work. These are the items most frequently used by artists in wood:

Wood carving chisels and gouges and parting tool.

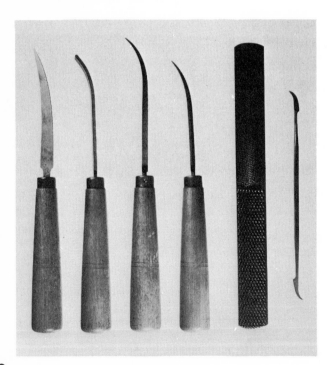

Bent rifflers used mainly for shaping and finishing wood, and a combination rasp and file with oval and flat sides.

Carpenter's Tools

Crosscut saw, so called because it is designed to cut across the grain. Used to remove excess wood from the block.

Coping saw, which has a thin blade for use on curves and in pierced relief work.

Plane, which is a chisel blade with an adjustable guide to regulate the extent of the cut. For shaving plane surfaces.

Also, a rule, a square, screwdriver, a brace with a selection of bits, pliers and marking gauge.

Woodcarving Tools

Chisels and gouges are the basic carving tools. Chisels have straight cutting edges which come in a range of sizes, the width depending on the size of the wood chip you want to remove. Chisels are of straight and skew types, the latter with a cutting edge set at a $45°$ angle to the shaft.

Gouges are the most frequently used tools for cutting away wood. They differ from chisels in that their cutting edges are curved in the shape of an arc, which varies in degree from semi-circular to nearly flat.

The Parting Tool, also known as the V-tool because of the shape of its cutting edge, cuts a V-like groove. The depth and width of this groove depends on the angle you choose.

The Veiner makes a shallow U-shaped groove and is favored for adding textural interest to the surface.

Rasps and Files are abrasive shaping tools useful for both removing wood and smoothing the surface prior to sand-papering and polishing. Their blade surfaces, which range from coarse to smooth, are available in varying sizes and shapes: flat, convex, round. The coarser the blade, the more wood you remove.

The Riffler is a small file which comes in many shapes, as it is intended to penetrate and finish off the awkward areas inaccessible to chisel and gouge.

The Scraper is a small piece of steel which, when rubbed over the wood surface, removes any teeth marks left by a too vigorous application of the rasp. Sometimes a piece of glass is used as a scraper.

The Mallet is a short-handled tool used like a hammer to drive the cutting tool into the wood. The smaller the cutting tool and the finer the work, the lighter the mallet.

The Surform file and plane are recently developed tools designed for shaping which are easy to use. The file, recommended for general shaping, has a blade flush with the front end of the tool for working into corners. The rear handle and front rest are formed to provide an easy grip and control. The plane is for heavy duty shaping and also has a front and rear handle. In addition to the standard blade furnished with both tools, you can buy a half-round blade for forming and smoothing circular and irregular surfaces. It will also remove stock rapidly. A fine-cut flat blade is available for forming hard, smooth surfaces.

Some artists in wood — particularly those working in the advanced styles — use power tools; other artists avoid them. That they have their place as time-savers, particularly when you are reducing a heavy piece of timber to size or drilling holes in a construction, is obvious. But whether or not you should attempt to use them as short-cuts to creativity is another question.

American sculptor and teacher John Hovannes maintains a full complement of electrical tools in his New York studio. But, he explains, "I permit my students to use them only after they have mastered the use of hand-tools. First it is necessary to experience the responsiveness and intractability of wood, to discover how wood and tools interact, and how the form emerges beneath your guiding hand. When you have mastered this human capability, then, in appropriate situations, you may draw on electric power."

The Surform plane is recommended for heavy duty shaping of the wood. The combination of rear and front handles makes it possible to work rapidly without losing control of direction. Photo courtesy of Stanley Tools.

The Smile, by Paul Gauguin. Woodcut on endgrain boxwood, printed in black, plate 4″ x 7³⁄₁₆″. Collection, The Museum of Modern Art, New York. Lillie P. Bliss Collection. Gauguin's woodcuts have strongly influenced the contemporary artists in this medium.

Sharpening Tools

Don't expect to spend all your hours at the workbench in continuous creativity. If you are to produce good work, you will devote many hours to sharpening your cutting tools to perfection — including the new ones you have just purchased. For this sharpening stones are required, of which the most popular are Arkansas (natural) and Carborundum (artificial). Also available commercially are oil-filled combination stones, one side coarse and the other side fine. India stone is widely used, and although it does not lend itself to rapid sharpening, it is durable and offers a very sharp cutting edge.

Before using, secure the stone to the workbench by fencing it in with small strips of wood. Then lightly apply a few drops of machine oil to the stone to prevent particles of steel from accumulating.

To sharpen a chisel, hold the tool firmly in one hand and with the fingers of the other press the bevel edge to the coarsest stone. Move the chisel back and forth in rapid, even motions, maintaining an even keel so one side of the bevel does not get more attention than the other. Turn the tool over for a few strokes to remove any grinding marks on the back. Now repeat the process on the smoother stone, ending by honing with a leather strop.

To sharpen a gouge, hold in the same manner as the chisel, but instead of rubbing the tool up and down the length of the stone, keep moving it from side to side, rotating it with a wrist movement, so that all of the outside cutting edge benefits equally from the sharpening. Then proceed to the inside or convex surface of the gouge by moving the tool back and forth a few times over a slipstone, which has a convex edge, and again conclude with a mild leather stropping.

To sharpen the knife, move the cutting edge back and forth over the stone, completing the sharpening on one side and then turning to the other. Stropping follows.

To sharpen the veiner, apply the same procedure you used for the chisel.

To sharpen the parting tool, treat it like two chisels combined. Do not try to refine the meeting point of the two sides to a fine sharpness, but consider it as a small gouge. For the inside use the concave-convex stone.

How often should you sharpen tools? Whenever they give

evidence of the least dullness. Indeed, making the honing of tools a matter-of-fact procedure each time you begin working is a good habit to acquire, as it will free you to focus your energies on creative work instead of expending them in a totally unnecessary battle.

A reminder: because tools are delicate instruments, they demand careful handling and maintenance. Never impatiently toss them onto the workbench or permit them to jumble together. Arrange them in a neat and consistent order so you can pick up one without disturbing the other. When you reach for the chisel, you don't want to inadvertently retrieve the gouge.

Finally, give some care to your sharpening stones. Wash and wipe them occasionally, and then feed their pores with a drop or two of oil.

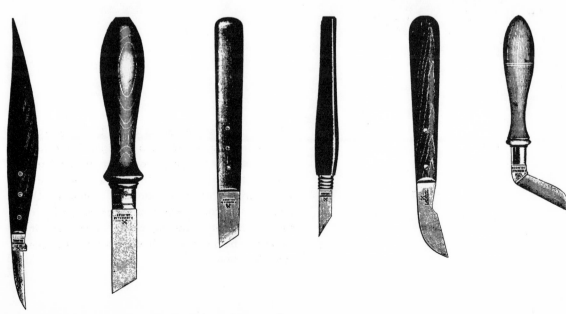

A selection of knives for cutting and carving wood.

Flying Angel, German, about 1480. Courtesy Wadsworth Atheneum, Hartford. 5½″ high. Characteristically Gothic is this polychromed wood carving of an angel holding a violin. The figure is believed to have been part of an altarpiece or chandelier. Observe the intricate surface carvings on arms and legs, the repetitive carving on the wings, and the contrasting bold strokes with which the hair has been given definition.

Guidelines for Using Carving Tools

Always secure the wood for your project to your workbench. This can be accomplished with a regular carpenter's vice, which is bolted to the underside of the work surface flush with the bench. Allowing more mobility is a swivel vice, which can be rotated and tilted at your convenience. Insert a scrap of wood between the jaws of the vice and your wood to prevent the latter from being marked or dented by the grip of the vice.

Not all sizes of wood can be conveniently held by a vice. To secure a medium to large block, simply attach to it with screws a strong, flat base. This base can then be fastened to the workbench with conventional C-clamps. You can also use clamps to secure the block directly to the bench, but use at least two or three. Free movement of the block will interfere with cutting.

Still another method of securing utilizes the bench screw. Protruding upward through a hole in the surface of the workbench, it screws into the base of the wood block or board.

The key to learning the use of carving tools lies in experimentation. No amount of reading will prove as instructive as finding out for yourself the capabilities and idiosyncrasies of each tool. The aim of this chapter is to get you to pick up the tools and start using them.

With the piece of wood firmly secured to the workbench, make an exploratory cut with knife or chisel to find the direction of the grain. If the cut is smooth, and the tool springs out clean, with the wood shaving or chip curling away from it, then you are working with the grain. If the tool sinks into the wood and produces a rough, uneven cut, or splits the chip, then you are going against the grain.

The importance of determining the grain becomes evident when you begin to remove excess wood by means of the stop cut and slice cut. These are basic actions which you will perform repeatedly in carving.

To make a stop cut, grasp the chisel or gouge firmly in one hand, at about mid-length, and drive it straight into the wood at a 90° angle by tapping it with a mallet. This first stroke is made against the grain. It severs the wood fibers but removes no wood. That is the task of the slice cut, which is made with the grain. At an angle of about 45°, drive the same tool into the wood to meet the bottom of the stop cut, and you will neatly remove a V-shaped piece of wood. Proceed with continuing slanting slice cuts to remove wood.

You may use the chisel or gouge interchangeably here, the chisel making a straight cut and the gouge a rounded one,

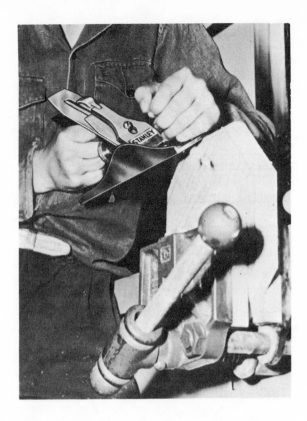

The chisel is held just above mid-length while a light tap of the mallet drives it along a defined path to remove wood in chips.

With the wood block secured firmly to the workbench, both hands are free to hold and guide the tool for planing the surface.

The edge of the chisel cuts into the wood and the bevel forces it apart. When working with the grain, the chip that rises will curl away from you.

CHOOSE CURVE DESIRED on chart — refer to top of page for size.
Refer to left hand columns for style (short bend — long bend — straight).

			$\frac{1''}{8}$	$\frac{3''}{16}$	$\frac{1''}{4}$	$\frac{5''}{16}$	$\frac{3''}{8}$	$\frac{7''}{16}$	$\frac{1''}{2}$	$\frac{9''}{16}$	$\frac{5''}{8}$	$\frac{3''}{4}$	$\frac{7''}{8}$	1 in.
21		1												
22	Right	2												
23	Left													
24	12	3												
25	13	4												
26	14	5												
27	15	6												
28	16	7												
29	17	8												
30	18	9												
31	19	10												
32	20	11												
44	42	41												
43	40	39												
	46	45												

Chart illustrating shapes and sizes of tools for carving wood.

David Hostetler, with chisel and mallet, blocking out a sculptural mass for one of his growing family of rough-hewn figures, while a completed pair look on enigmatically. Perhaps as a carry-over from his earlier abstract style, Hostetler gives a minimum of definition to the features, achieves accent by applying paint to indicate hair and gown. As associate professor at Ohio University, he has set up his studio on the livestock farm where he lives with his family. Photo courtesy of the Sculpture Center.

the degree of roundness determined by the degree of curvature of the cutting edge. Experiment by varying the slant of the slice cuts. Note different effects of gouge and chisel — and that with a gouge you can cut across the grain without tearing the wood.

You may also use the chisel to carve flat planes along an even path, provided you work with the grain. The chisel's sharp edge cuts into the wood, while its bevel forces the wood apart, thus rapidly removing wood in chips and shavings.

In another experiment, begin with a large, semi-circular gouge, making deep cuts at sharp angles. This quickly removes the excess wood not necessary to your image or design. As the broad outline begins to emerge, proceed with smaller, less curved gouges, positioning them at lower and lower angles to the wood, and making cuts which are less and less pronounced.

With the veining tool, carve a shallow vein along the surface of the wood, and notice how this slightest of grooves can function decoratively.

Cutting is one way of removing wood; abrasion with rasp or file is another. When using the rasp, you file away the wood, in either a shaping or smoothing action. Holding a coarse rasp at both ends, guide the flat side along the edge of the wood in even strokes until the sharp angle has been reduced to a curve. Then work toward a gentle, smooth finish by using a smaller, finer rasp. Note how rasps can be used to give a relatively smooth finish to an entire project in this way. Always test rasps on the same kind of wood as your project. When dull, the rasp may mark and scratch the wood.

When you have cut into the wood an area which is inaccessible to the rasp or file, reach in with a riffler to complete the smoothing operation.

To repeat: knowing which tool to pick up for a specific action comes with experience. At the beginning, work with a few tools — knife, chisel, gouge, rasp, mallet — and get to know them well. Experiment by cutting and filing at different angles, on different woods. And note what happens. Your goal is not to learn a mechanical operation where fixed rules are necessary, but to develop work habits that will enable you to create in wood.

A word of caution. Carving tools are sharp. Never hold a piece of wood in one hand while carving with the other. Secure it to the work bench.

Never attempt to grab a falling tool. Serious cuts can result.

Pick up tools by the handle and in no other way.

Protect your eyes with protective glasses when rapidly carving away excess wood from a large block.

When you begin to feel tired, relax for a while, preferably away from the workbench. Fatigue causes accidents — and it also causes you to ruin the work over which you have been toiling. It's a great temptation to stick with a project as it nears completion. Avoid it. This kind of thinking leads to short-cuts and careless workmanship which have no place in your work of art.

Pierced Hemisphere (Telstar), by Barbara Hepworth. 1963. Guarea wood, 36½″ high. Courtesy Marlborough-Gerson Gallery, New York.

Golem, Hugh Townley. 1956. Maple, walnut, ebony and amaranth. 40″ high. Collection of the Whitney Museum of American Art, gift of the New York Foundation.

Painted Relief, by Ben Nicholson. 1939. Synthetic board mounted on plywood, painted. 32⅞" x 45". Collection, The Museum of Modern Art, New York. Gift of H. S. Ede and the artist. In this classicly simple relief, the sections of board mounted on the plywood background have been cut and painted with gem-like precision according to a carefully worked-out design. Compare this work with one of the traditional reliefs illustrated in this book to grasp the wide range of possibilities open to the artist in wood within a specific process.

Relief Carving

In relief carving, the image or design stands out "in relief" against the sunken background which has been cut away. Effects of light and shadow are realized by means of the varying depths and the angles at which the wood is carved.

The type of wood selected for relief carving should depend on the design. For finely detailed work, a close-grained hardwood is advisable; whereas softwoods can be worked easily to produce simpler, bolder and less sharply articulated images.

Traditionally, relief work is classified in three ways. High relief comes closest to attaining the three-dimensional reality of sculpture. The image stands out distinctly from the background, but without being detached from it.

In low or bas relief, the contrast between image and background is least marked. When the design is sunk entirely into the surface, it is termed hollow relief, or intaglio. In this book hollow relief is treated as a separate technique called incised carving. The techniques appropriate to high relief are similar to those of carving in the round and are covered in the section on sculpture.

For low relief carving, a board and the simplest of carving tools will suffice. Create a design compatible with the character and thickness of the board and transfer it to the wood. Once you have established the depth of the design, never exceed it. Gradually work inwards from the outline of the design, removing excess wood with chisel and gouge. Soon the broad outlines of the design will appear "in relief." With finer gouges approach closer to the outline, working to achieve a neat and clean demarcation between image and background. Proceed now to detail work within the outline, making even the deepest cuts less deep than the sunken background.

Child, by E. Glicenstein. 1928. Walnut relief carving, 13½" x 12½". Collection of Emanuel Romano. This sculptural relief fills out the four sides of the square, and even the areas between limb and torso have been given substance and form by the artist. The surface has been roughly textured with the gouge except for the flat areas which are the original surface of the wood block.

When you have completed carving within the outline, you may want to add light-and-shadow interest to the outer edges of the image by undercutting — that is, slightly cutting away wood so that the top edge of the image overlaps the background.

Whether or not you decide to "soften" the sharp outline of the image will depend on what effect you intend. In an abstract design, the sharp contrast between image and background may considerably enhance the visual impact. When the image is representational, you may want to round the edging somewhat.

Generally, it is a good idea to progress from low relief to high relief. The latter technique encourages more complex designs but demands many of the skills required for carving in the round. With low relief, on the other hand, you can obtain interesting results fairly early in your progress, thus building up a nice capital of self-confidence.

Nor should low relief, because of its comparative simplicity, be considered the more lowly technique. The panel of Hesire, carved in low relief in 2800 B.C. to adorn the tomb of a young Egyptian noble, remains an outstanding representation of the human figure, its simple lines conveying an impression of dignity and strength undiminished by the passing centuries. In modern art, the reliefs of Jean Arp also testify to the powerful results which the artist can realize with minimal means.

As you develop skill with tools, the temptation to add detail for its own sake to your relief, or because you want to dis-

play your skills, may seem overpowering at times. Resist it. For a few days you may enjoy displaying this proof of your expertise. But in the long run the fancy ornamentation will only detract from enjoyment of the piece as a work of art. In carving as in many forms of art, "Less is more."

A note about the relief technique favored by some modern artists. In the Arp illustrated in this book, the motif or design, instead of being carved from the same board as the background, has been carved from a separate piece of wood and mounted on the panel. This technique, which permits the use of contrasting woods, is sometimes considered a form of assemblage and is treated further in the chapter under that heading. However, the visual effect is achieved by means of contrasting depth, as in relief.

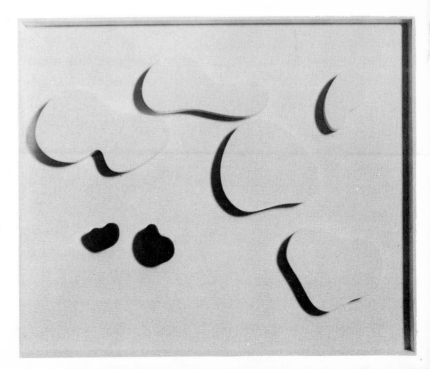

Variation 2: Constellation with Five White and Two Black Forms, by Jean Arp. Painted wood relief, 27⅝" x 33½" x 1½". Collection, The Museum of Modern Art, New York. The Sidney and Harriet Janis Collection.

Incised and Chip Carving

Like relief work, incised carving depends for effect on attaining contrasting depths in the wood. Whereas in low and high relief carving this contrast is realized by cutting away the background area, in incised carving the technique is just the opposite. The background level is left undisturbed, while the design is cut into it and sunk beneath the surface.

Run your hand over a low relief carving and you will sense the image or design by means of the wood which has been raised above the sunken background. Run your hand over an incised carving, and you will read the design by means of the lines and hollows carved in the surface.

Incised carving is one of the easiest of the woodworking techniques. With softwoods like cedar and redwood you can produce encouraging results with a minimum of expertise. The woods with dramatic grain patterns should generally be avoided. Your design will be recessed beneath the surface, and the strength and boldness of grain tends to obscure the light-and-shadow values of the carving.

Establish your design so that the primary lines go across the grain of the wood. For tools, experiment with carving knife, parting tool, chisel and gouge. The hollows in incised carving may be varied in texture according to the tools you use and the angle at which the cuts are made. Depending upon the design, you may desire a smooth trough or a groove incised with repeated geometric cuts.

Chip carving may be considered as a form of incised carving, usually associated with repetitious and geometric patterns. Again the wood should be as straight-grained and unassertive as possible in order not to disturb the design pattern. A straight or skew chisel are all you need for conventional chip carving. It is a technique more used for decorative effect than for artistic purposes.

An example of chip carving put to practical use. Courtesy Cepelia Corporation.

Mask, Kifwebe, Songe Tribe (Congo). Photo courtesy Galerie Kamer, Inc., New York. A fine example of the disciplined use of incised carving is provided by this magnificent ceremonial mask from the Congo. Note how the parellel lines are contained within geometric forms. Masks such as this were very influential in the work of Picasso, Matisse and Braque during the beginning of Cubism.

Pierced Carving

Both pierced and high relief carving are illustrated in this pair of Japanese 19th century panels, which show two *shishi* perched on rockwork and surrounded by flowering peonies. The design continues on the reverse side of the 41⅜" high panels. (Courtesy of Parke-Bernet Galleries.)

Imagine for a moment that you could completely detach a low relief carving from its background and mount it on a base to stand alone. With the design thus silhouetted in space, you could view it from all sides, enjoying the delicate play of light through the openings in the design. That would be a pierced carving, also known as fretwork.

Lacking the support of a background, the pierced carving must rely for its strength on the wood, which must be sufficiently hard to withstand toolwork and prevent warping, and on the design, which should be conceived to provide a network of reinforcing connections. For example, the design may call for an arm extended in space, a sure invitation to breakage. By rethinking the design so that the end of the arm connects with another point in the design, this hazard is avoided.

Once you have decided that your design lends itself to pierced carving and have transferred it to the panel, begin to carve away the excess wood from around the outline. To carve within the outline, first drill holes at the appropriate points to permit access to the jigsaw.

Before beginning the detailed and delicate toolwork needed to complete the pierced carving, obtain some support that will make your job easier. With thin wire nails, attach the carving to the workbench or a flat board. Remember that pierced carving can't be rushed. It demands patience and self-discipline. When you feel your hand growing heavy, or your grip on the tool tightening, take a break.

Figures of Saints, German. 18th Century, 34½" high.
Courtesy of Parke-Bernet Galleries, New York.

Sculpture

Sculpture, or carving in the round, presents a three-dimensional form visually accessible from any side or angle. Unlike the relief, where the image is still conveyed by essentially linear means, the carving in the round is realized by the manipulation and arrangement of mass and volume. To clarify this distinction between line and volume, note the comparative ease with which you can make a pen or pencil sketch of a relief — and the difficulty you experience when attempting to render by the same means your impression of a sculpture, where the qualities of depth and space are basic to the medium.

This does not mean that your carving in the round should not be combined with other techniques. In many of the illustrations included here you will note the application of incised and relief carving to a sculptural mass. In contemporary artistry in wood, the tendency to achieve effect by combining multiple techniques is particularly pronounced.

Mother and Child, by E. Glicenstein. 1932. Walnut, 21" x 10" x 10". Collection of Emanuel Romano and Hugo Dreyfuss. The size of the block from which this work was carved is the same as that of the finished piece. The end of the block can be clearly seen at the end of the child's nose and the back of the mother's head in the bronze cast, and at the top of the mother's head in the original wood. Very little wood was removed to create this work, an outstanding example of the relief carving principle applied to sculpture. Notice that the motif is raised a very limited degree.

The same sculpture cast in bronze, and showing the opposite side. Many bronzes exhibited in museums are cast from the original wood carvings.

To succeed in wood sculpture you must think in the round as well as work in the round. One way to develop this skill is by carving several abstract elementary forms in the round, "walking around them" with your mind's eye while you work, and developing a sense of proportion applicable, not just to a frontal view, but to the whole.

Experiment with the form of one of the abstract carvings reproduced here. Without attempting to reproduce it, take it as a starting point for developing your own carving in the round. Improvise and allow free play to your imagination as you proceed. Whether your work turns out to be round, oblong, hollow or solid, rough or smooth, is unimportant. Your goal is to train your mind and your senses to respond in three dimensions.

Explore the possibilities of the wood block, concentrate on simple forms, attempting to reveal them by removing as little of the wood as possible. Let your first collection of "works" be a group of elemental forms, leaving some in the rough state, refining others to a fine smoothness. Don't worry about using the correct tool for each motion. Experiment, discover, work with the wood in complete freedom. In this way you possess your medium, find out what is right for you. Then move on to specific designs drawn on the block.

Practically any wood will lend itself to some kind of carving in the round, the criterion of choice being whether or not its characteristics are appropriate to the realization of the design. Whatever the wood, mount the block in such a way that you can follow the grain when carving. First examine the grain, then draw the front and side views on the block, positioning the block so you can work from the top downwards.

To keep your hands free for gouge and mallet, secure the wood block to a board with screws. Fasten the board to your workbench with clamps or vise. (See section on Tools).

Examine the image or design you have drawn on the block. Is it cramped? Then the block is too small for the concept. Or perhaps you have exaggerated the design to fill out the block. By thinking the design in terms of the block, you assure better proportions for the sculpture. Alternatively, you may have a block cut to the size necessary for a specific design. If you are satisfied with the rightness of the drawing, take up a small gouge and rough in the outline on the block. From this point on, your sculptural task will be to make the form reveal itself by removing excess wood.

If the block is small, remove the excess wood farthest from the outline with a coping saw; with a crosscut or ripsaw if the block is large. Use a large gouge for further roughing out, still keeping your distance from the outline. If you feel uncomfortable with the saw, do all the roughing out with a gouge. Many sculptors do.

Continue blocking out the planes on all sides until the contours of the design or image begin to emerge. Do not interrupt this all-around approach to attempt finishing off one side in your impatience to see what it will be like. Think

Angel of Annunciation, Italian, about 1500. Poly-chromed walnut, 43" high. Courtesy, Wadsworth Atheneum, Hartford.

Two Forms by Henry Moore. 1934. Pynkado wood, 11" x 17¾" on irregular oak base, 21" x 12½". Collection, The Museum of Modern Art, New York, Sir Michael Sadler Fund. Moore makes excellent use of space to build an interesting relationship between his two curved forms.

Economy of means in David Hostetler's sculpture does nothing to diminish its life-like stance. Photo by Jon Webb; courtesy of the Sculpture Center.

American sculptor John Hovannes cutting away wood with chisel and mallet. A hydraulic power arm controls the direction of the wood block. While Hovannes believes the sculptor should "use any kind of tools that help him achieve his goal," he counsels his students to "stay away from power tools until you have mastered the use of hand tools. Unless you can feel what you are doing, you're in danger of being carried away by the ease with which wood can be removed."

Mitsogo Fetish, Gabon. 15″ high. Courtesy Galerie Kamer, Inc. New York. We are grateful that this was rescued before further decay.

Nude, by John Hovannes. Teakwood. 30″ high. Courtesy of the artist. The close straight grain of teakwood is used to excellent advantage to define the fluid lines of the figure.

Ship's Figurehead from Nantucket, American, circa 1820, artist unknown. The Newark Museum. With their carvings of figureheads for America's sailing vessels, the New England artists in wood take us into the poetic world of Hawthorne and Melville. The weathered condition of the wood only serves to enhance its beauty. This 42″ high carving from Nantucket, Mass., may have been intended as a likeness of the young Benjamin Franklin.

before you cut, always keeping in mind your vision of the completed work.

Now go over the entire surface again — but with progressively smaller and flatter gouges, all the while lowering the angle at which you cut. Proceeding now with deliberation and caution, you remove tiny chips with light hand blows on the gouge, until you seem to be smoothing the surface instead of cutting into it. Leave detail work for last.

Additional shaping and smoothing with rasp and riffler will also remove tool marks and give increased visibility to the grain. But use these abrading tools with caution. Be sure they do not remove more wood than you intend. And note the many sculptures illustrated in these pages where the tool marks have been retained as an integral part of the surface design.

For further smoothing, apply a scraper and then sandpaper. Smoothing, it should be noted, is a time-consuming and painstaking task. And you do not necessarily want to give each sculpture a smooth, sleek surface. Certainly you did not expend all that effort to produce an object that looks as if it had been made by machine in a factory!

Helpful hints for carving in the round:

Practice observing people, animals, objects as elemental sculptural forms. With no regard for detail, make rough sketches of a bird, fish, a cat, reducing them to the broadest outlines. When you have simplified the sketch to the degree where it is the merest suggestion of the representational image, outline it on the wood block for carving. In carving these forms which hover between the representational and the abstract, you will learn to focus on the essential elements of your carving in the round — and in the process produce some interesting, stylized work.

There's nothing wrong with imitation. Working from any of the illustrations in this book, you will gain valuable experience in working wood in different ways. But don't make your ability to slavishly imitate a measure of success. You don't want to turn into a machine. Instead, when you see a carving which stimulates you, try to express the image or design in your own fashion, using the original as a springboard to launch you into action.

Develop your sense of tactile awareness. Learn to relate what you see with what you experience with your hands. Experiment by running your hands slowly over objects with different shapes and surfaces, wood and other materials. This tactile understanding will aid you to control the proportions of your work and enhance your ability to guide tools to perform the desired cutting and smoothing actions.

Inlay

Inlay is used to decorate architectural features such as paneling and molding and also to create "pictures" which can be hung on the wall. When applied to furniture, it is called marquetry. Basically inlay is achieved by combining different kinds of wood in geometrical, abstract, floral or other patterns, or to tell a story as in the inlay illustrated.

Lait Sterilize, craftsman unknown, after a poster by T. Steinlen, wood inlay, 14" x 12½". Collection Mrs. Florence Hamm; photo by Ken Eargle. The inlay originated sometime in the 14th century when artists sought ways to satisfy the new yearning for beauty and elegance then arising in Europe. The technique was soon taken up by craftsmen and became popular in America as a means of achieving ornamental and pictorial effects in wood with comparatively little effort. In this example, note how the different woods have been laid into the background, using the wood grain and color to define the elements of the picture.

The woods are usually of veneer thickness, and the colors and patterns of the woods determine the effect. Don't make your first inlay part of a larger work — experiment. First draw the design on paper, making cut-outs of the individual parts. Work with these cut-outs until you get a pattern or image that pleases you.

Keep one copy of the total design intact and use it as a guide for hollowing out with your carving tools the surface area of a panel into which you will later fit the individual pieces of wood.

Now cut to the same size as your cut-outs pieces of wood of different patterns and colors, according to the effect at which you are aiming. When all the pieces have been carved, you have what appears to be the elements of a jig-saw puzzle. Wedge them into the area which has been hollowed out of the panel as dictated by the design.

Or, instead of cutting away a hollowed-out ground to contain the pieces, merely cut a frame for your design from a sheet of wood the same thickness as the inlay. With glue, attach both the frame and the inlay to a solid backing about 1" thick.

Understandably, to be able to "lay in" the individual pieces so they fit neatly, careful and exact cutting is essential. Selective staining of pieces cut from one kind of wood can aid in achieving contrast. However, the challenge and reward are greater if you don't resort to staining but work with different wood colors and patterns.

Woodcuts

There are few museums today without their treasure of fine woodcut prints. Yet this oldest of printing processes is inexpensive and accessible to anyone with a few cutting tools, a nondescript piece of board to use as a wood block, and some paper and printing ink.

Head of a Young Woman, by Pablo Picasso. 1933.
Woodcut printed in black. 20¼" x 13½". Collection,
The Museum of Modern Art, New York. Abby Aldrich
Rockefeller Fund.

Woodcutting is a relief process. You draw your composition directly onto the surface of the wood block, raising it — or bringing it into relief — by cutting away the wood between the lines and around the area you desire to print. The lines or areas which remain in relief are called black, or positive. The lines or areas you cut away are called white, or negative.

Ink is spread on these raised lines and areas, and a piece of paper placed over the wood block. When pressure is applied to the paper, the design is transferred from the block to the paper, thereby creating a woodcut print. You may make just one impression from the wood block, or you may want to print several, varying the inking procedure, the quality of the paper, and the pressure applied, until you arrive at the exact combination of values for a fine print. Whether you make five or fifteen impressions from the one block, each is considered an original work of art.

Often as many as three individuals are involved in creating woodcut prints: the artist who draws the design on the wood block, the carver who cuts away wood to bring the design into relief, and the printer. Generally, contemporary artists prefer to take complete responsibility for the process, and it is this total approach to the woodcut which is also most rewarding for the beginner. You control quality every inch of the way, can experiment, modifying each step and testing results as you proceed — and you experience the joy of creating woodcut prints which carry the authentic stamp of your workmanship.

What kind of wood should you use? Whatever kinds you can lay your hands on, including pieces of packing crates! When purchasing, ask for blocks that have been cut parallel to the tree and in the direction of the grain. Such a cut is termed plankwood or side wood. If you have a choice, experiment with fir, pine, beech, maple, poplar, birch — and plywood. The one restriction is that the wood be thick enough to enable you to carve in enough depth to achieve clear relief.

Don't limit your search to perfect pieces of wood (knots can produce interesting design effects); and don't reduce to a uniform smoothness pieces with a coarsely textured surface. First try using woods with their personalities intact, observe the kind of prints you produce with different woods, and add them to your repertoire of woodcut capabilities, to be selected when an appropriate subject or design comes alone.

Your woodcutting tools are the knife, V-tool, gouge, chisel and mallet. To print, you need oil or water inks, a brush for applying the ink, paper, and a 6" wide by 1½" diameter printing roller.

Conceive your design in terms of the black-and-white woodcut as a specific medium. Remember that the lines or areas where you cut away wood will appear white on your impression. The lines or areas which you leave raised above the sunken background, by cutting away wood between and around them, will print in black. At first, aim for strong, simple contrasts.

Sketching the design on paper and then transferring it to the wood block is an acceptable procedure. But drawing it directly onto the block with a felt-tipped pen is preferable, since it encourages you to incorporate the wood grain into the design. Also, while woodcut effects may appear linear, they are arrived at, not by incising the wood in a continuous, flowing line as in a drawing, with the knife serving as the equivalent of a pen, but rather by cutting away the wood as in sculpture, where the line is achieved by a succession of individual cutting actions.

Strive to cut along the grain instead of across it. And select tools for ease of use. Don't tire yourself making parallel lines with a knife when a V-tool will do the job more rapidly.

When you have completed cutting away wood, wipe off the block with benzine and a damp cloth and allow to dry. Then prepare the printing roller to apply ink to the block. This is done in a rather indirect procedure. First cover a section of your workbench with a piece of plate glass. With a spatula or brush, spread printing ink on the glass and then distribute it evenly with the roller. Your objective is to cover the roller evenly with ink. To apply the ink to the block, move the roller in rapid even strokes over the raised, or printing surface, raising it after each stroke.

Having completed the inking process, place the paper on the block, securing it in position with a few weights. You are now ready to apply pressure to the paper and print. The most effective — and simplest — method is by rubbing the surface with a hard, rounded object, such as a spoon.

By varying the pressure applied to different areas of the paper, you can vary the tonal values of sections of the print, making one deep black, the other grey. Similarly, you can vary the effects of successive impressions. These refinements are not available when you depend on a hand press.

It's a good idea to make proof prints — that is, prints of your "work in progress" before completing the design. This permits you to see how your work will print before you have committed the wood block completely. Newsprint or wrapping paper is adequate for proof prints. Also, when printing, don't hesitate to lift a bit of the paper and sneak a look. That way you can judge where you are applying too much pressure — or not enough — to get the desired tonal values. For best printing results, dampen paper slightly with a sponge. For quality presentation prints, select a good drawing paper.

An easy way to get two-color prints is with a colored paper and/or colored ink. Experiment using the same procedures as outlined for black and white.

To make true color woodcuts, however, you need an additional block for each color. Grind the pigments in water and apply to the block like a paste.

Sign your prints and number them 1/10 or 8/10, etc., indicating the first or eighth print of a total of ten.

Gerson as a Pilgrim, artist unknown, circa 1490. Woodcut. Photo courtesy Kennedy Galleries, New York.

Church, by Lionel Feininger. Woodcut. 11¼" x 12".
Courtesy Martin Gordon Gallery.

Death of Adonis, by Luca Cambiaso (1527-1585). Woodcut, 10¼" x 12". Courtesy Kennedy Galleries.

Nach Dem Fang, by Max Pechstein. 1923. Woodcut, 15¾" x 12½". Courtesy Martin Gordon Gallery.

Rooster, by Emanuel Romano. Woodcut, mahogany. 12" x 9".

Wooden Floating Compression Column, by Kenneth Snelson. 1948. Courtesy of Dwan Gallery, New York. Balance, tension, grace and strength are expressed in this 11″ x 5″ construction of wood and wire. The key to the success of many contemporary constructions lies not in the variety of kinds and shapes of wood that are brought together but rather in the imagination and skill with which a few pieces are assembled to create a new image.

Assemblage and Construction

In carving, you arrive at the intended image or design by removing excess wood. In assemblage and construction, on the other hand, you reach your goal by adding one piece of wood to another, literally building up to the total effect.

Construction is an ancient technique, used by the Egyptians when total carving was impractical — to add extended limbs to a standing figure, for example. But modern artists give the term a different meaning. Instead of resorting to construction as a means of overcoming an obstacle in carving, they justify it as a unique woodworking process yielding its own esthetic rewards.

An assemblage or construction may be representational or abstract, built from natural wood, plywood or found timber. The pieces may be joined by glue, nails, screws, dowels, wire or simple dovetailing. But while imposing few material and working limitations, the assemblage or construction which is to succeed as a work of art demands much thought and careful planning.

Rocking Chair by Anne Arnold. 1962. 39″ high x 44″ x 13″. Courtesy Fischbach Gallery. Pine planks, a saw, chisel, glue and dowels are the elements of this very human construction. Note how the visible tool marks lend character and expression to the face, while the arms, legs and feet remain highly stylized.

The Palace at 4 A.M. by Alberto Giacometti, 1932-33. Construction in wood, glass, wire, string. 25″ x 28¼″ x 15¾″. Collection, The Museum of Modern Art, New York. Giocometti's *Palace* achieves its Surrealist effect with a classical economy of means.

The construction offers a way of defining space not available to the sculptor. Experiment by building out of wood strips two identical triangles. Mount them on a wood base a few inches apart and display them so that light projects their combined shadows on a wall or rear panel. Secure the triangles to the base so that they may be turned sufficiently to capture varying light patterns. Experiment with your mounted triangles further by connecting them with tautly drawn wire at each of the three points, and note the space you have now enclosed as part of the work. Seemingly an elementary exercise, it will reveal some of the exciting possibilities of construction.

Observe how a few pieces of wood and wire combine imaginatively in Giacometti's *Palace at Four A.M.* to build a mood. For contrast, note the manner in which Anne Arnold has joined individual pieces of wood to express the human form in *Rocking Chair.*

Varied means are used to join pieces of wood in construction, most of them requiring only ordinary carpenter's tools and skills. What is important is that the means be appropriate to the ends. A bold display of screws and bolts and heavy wire may add to the impression of power and stability you want to convey in one work. In another, you may want to conceal the joining entirely by depending on one of the wood glues. Glass, steel, synthetics of all kinds may be incorporated into the construction — but only if they help to make the intended statement.

Sky Cathedral, by Louise Nevelson. Assemblage: wood construction painted black, 11′ 3½″ x 10′ ¼″ x 1′6″. Collection, The Museum of Modern Art, New York. Gift of Mr. and Mrs. Ben Mildwoff. In this masterwork of assemblage and construction, individual boxes frame arrangements of abstract forms made up of pieces of wood discarded from the workbench and strips of old carpets. Painted black throughout, the composition gathers power and mystery from the subtle build-up of detail in which no two forms are exactly alike.

Sculpture in the Form of a Trowel Stuck in the Ground,
by Claes Oldenburg, 1970. Wood. 46″ x 29¾″ x 24″.
Courtesy Sidney Janis Gallery, New York.

An individual form of assemblage and construction is the "collage," a term derived from the French word for pasting or mounting. The technique first surfaced in the art world in the Paris of 1912, when Picasso and Braque, instead of painting imitation newspapers, oilcloth and fabrics, stuck pieces of the original materials on their work. German artist Kurt Schwitters, perhaps the greatest of the collage builders, soon carried the technique beyond verisimilitude and into fantasy and abstraction, where pleasing arrangements of shapes and colors became ends in themselves.

The collage offers rich opportunities for the play of imagination and intellect. Against a variety of panels ranging from fine grade board to segments of packing crates, position horizontal and vertical strips of wood. Carve a number of geometric forms and arrange these elements on the background panel of your collage in the manner of the Surrealists, letting your subconscious dictate what goes where. Combine shapes carved from different woods so that each sets off the color and texture of the other. You may even want to recall the painterly origins of the collage by building a simple frame for your work.

Chances are you will use glue in assemblage and construction. Among the recommended commercial products are Elmer's Glue-All, which has a good bind, is quick-setting, and dries clear; waterproof glue, for heavy-duty use in constructions designed for the out-of-doors; and Weldwood cement for bonding laminates.

This beechwood bench by a contemporary Polish craftsman is carved in broad outlines with the tool marks retained for surface interest. Courtesy Cepelia Corporation.

Practical Artistry in Wood

Throughout history, the practical has offered the occasion for the beautiful. In fashioning his tools, utensils, weapons, furniture, the artist and craftsman at the same time sought to express their sense of form and color, and to give to these objects a value beyond the utilitarian. They saw no reason why items of daily use should not also delight the eye and be pleasing to touch.

Today, this bond which united the practical and beautiful has dissolved under the impact of mass production. Even objects labeled "hand made" bear the stamp of the machine! Think of the items made of wood you have seen in gift and souvenir shops. Although many come from far-off places, they might just as well have been manufactured in one factory. Any marks of individuality have been ruthlessly eliminated.

One aim of this book is to bring you into touch with the great woodworking tradition, where imagination, individuality and a sense of beauty loom more importantly than concern over what some mysterious "public" out there will buy. A folding wood screen with incised carving of your own design, a wood box in which to store personal treasures, a child's crib, a salt and pepper set, a wood bowl —

these can serve as vehicles for the expression of your creativity and craftsmanship. Simple objects all, they can be raised far above the level of the trite and "craftsy" by your determination to "be yourself" as an artist in wood.

In the beginning, when carving objects for use, such as utensils, aim for the simplest of designs. As the form emerges from the wood, test it for weight, balance, function. Make the fullest possible use of the characteristics of the wood. Use ornamentation to reinforce the overall design, not to make the object "arty."

Live for a few days with your carvings in a near-finished state, testing with eye and hand their lines and proportions. You may find that a little rounding off, a slight accenting of a plane, is all that is needed to give a sense of completeness. Experiment with various woods — walnut, maple, birch, where the total effect depends on shape and contour rather than grain; then turn to the woods where the strong grain pattern dictates the line to follow.

The repeated motif characteristic of chip carving is used to decorative effect in this shelf. Courtesy Cepelia Corporation.

Chess Set (Boxwood), by Max Ernst. About 1945.
Courtesy Philadelphia Museum of Art.

Horse and Rider, carved wood. Courtesy Rowland's Antiques, Buckingham, Bucks County, Pa. This 5'22" x 5'2" painted wood carving served as an inn sign, an early form of advertising which offered to the woodcarver an opportunity to put his skills to practical use.

Contemporary wood chest with relief paneling. Courtesy Cepelia Corporation.

To carve a bowl, choose a block of appropriate size. With a fairly large gouge, begin to hollow out the inside, working from top to bottom, and being careful to control symmetry all around. You can cut off the main masses of wood from the outside with a coping saw and then, with the bowl upside down, cut away excess wood with a large gouge until the contour emerges. Proceed with a smaller, flatter gouge, finishing off with standpaper.

Until factory-produced products flooded the market, the making of furniture presented many opportunities for creativity to the woodcarver. Medieval household and ecclesiastical furniture featured elaborately carved panels, and during the Renaissance nobles and wealthy merchants competed strenuously for the services of the artist-craftsman whose shop could turn out the most intricately carved and embellished wood chest. Fine woodcarving was highly appreciated in early American homes, where it appeared on paneling, stairways, fireplaces and on the walnut, mahogany and pine furniture.

In most American furniture carving, the design consists of a repetition of lines and forms with occasional variations. Used sparingly and with deliberate severity, ornamental carving can enhance your home. Unfortunately, examples of good household and furniture carving are hard to come by. Many of the antiques displayed in shops display an excess of ornamentation and should not be taken as examples.

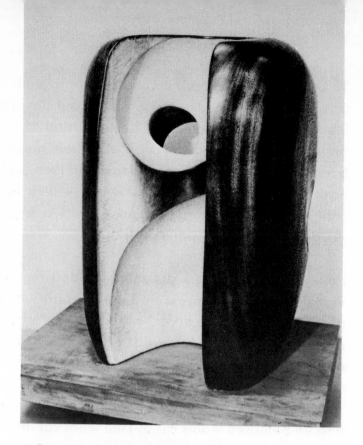

Madonna and Child, Tuscan, early 14th century. Polychromed wood, 47½" high. Courtesy of Parke-Bernet Galleries. Gothic and Renaissance sculptors were fond of applying flat, unmodulated earth colors to the surface of their sculpture. Called Polychroming, this technique was popular in ancient civilizations as well as among primitive peoples.

Hollow Form (Penwith), by Barbara Hepworth. 1955-56. Lagos wood, partly painted. 35⅜" x 25⅞" x 25⅝", attached to base. Collection, The Museum of Modern Art, New York. Gift of Dr. and Mrs. Arthur Lejwa. Openings in the planes which permit the light to come through and thus add another dimension to the sculpture are frequently used by this British artist. Note that the paint serves the purpose of accentuating the richness of the wood.

Finishing

There are two reasons for applying a finish to your otherwise completed work. One is to preserve it against the inroads of dust and dirt. And unless it is sealed with some kind of preservative, climatic change, through expansion and contraction, will cause it to crack or split. Also, the untreated wood surface is generally too absorbent to resist stain. The second justification for finishing is that the additional treatment may enhance or reinforce the impact of the work.

Actually, the finishing process begins before you put away your tools, when you decide whether or not to erase all evidence of tool marks by abrasion with rasp, riffler and scraper. A further application with sandpaper gives a fine, smooth finish. If you want to retain the drama of tool marks, forget about sandpapering.

To simply preserve wood without changing its natural appearance, apply a light coating of linseed oil. After it has dried, rub the surface with fine steel wool. Finish with a few coats of clear floor or furniture wax. If the work is to stand out-of-doors, it will need coating and rubbing with raw linseed oil at regular intervals.

You can also give your work the appearance of minimum finish by applying a dull lacquer. This protects the wood, provides a surface that repels water and resists scratches, and doesn't affect the wood color or grain. Do not let the lacquer accumulate on the surface, as it may produce an unintended roughness. To avoid this kind of imperfection, go over the surface with fine steel wool and a cloth after each application.

Remember that the surface of the work plays a vital role in the impression it conveys. A high gloss may well enhance the lines of a small, delicate figure but be hopelessly out of place on a strong and massive abstract. When you polish, you change the personality of the work, which is fine, provided it is your intention.

An even more basic change takes place when you apply a colored oil-base stain. These ready-made stains are commercially available in several transparent colors and may be applied in light, rapid strokes, as though you were painting the surface of the wood. Stains, however, do not coat the wood — they penetrate into it. Several applications may be needed to achieve the desired tone. Since stains are almost impossible to remove, it's advisable to experiment on a scrap of wood of the same kind as the project. After staining, follow the preservative and polishing techniques previously discussed. An occasional waxing or oiling will do much to preserve your work.

Should you paint your carving or construction? Only you can decide. Certainly there's ample precedent. The ancient Egyptians, the Gothic woodcarvers, the American Indian and the craftsmen who made the figureheads for the nation's sailing vessels, all sought to increase the interest of their work by the addition of color. Today, the bright, gaudy, satirical figures of Marisol sport color uninhibitedly; while Louise Nevelson's *Sky Cathedral* towers mysteriously beneath a coat of black paint.

But don't use color until you have weighed its negative effects. Paint generally conceals the grain, and jolts the eye by interfering with the natural beauty of wood. It is a value that is "added on" to the carving or construction, not one that is developed out of the primary material.

On the positive side, color can contribute gaiety, humor, contrast to small wood carvings of animals, for example; and when boldly applied to a construction, paint can build up to striking effects, creating impressions of solidity, lightness, movement.

There are no hard and fast rules on using color, and only your artist's eye, your sense of what is "right" for the individual project can guide you. Try two experiments.

(1) Carve a simple, stylized animal form, as though you were making a toy for a child. Then accent individual parts with acrylic or enamel paint. In selecting colors, don't aim

for realism but for an overall effect of gaiety and spontaneity. If this experiment seems too child-like, remember that sculptor Alexander Calder first won recognition as a maker of wood toys for his now famous miniature circus.

(2) Create a surface relief from plywood, painting a rectangular background one solid color. Now carve circular cut-outs in various sizes from a second plywood sheet. Paint the cut-outs in contrasting or complementary colors. When the paint has dried, position one or more of the cut-outs on the panel, trying various arrangements until satisfied. Then finalize your assembly with glue and frame it.

Noon, by John Hovannes, contemporary American. 1955. African mahogany. Courtesy of the artist. Mr. Hovannes first made a small sketch, photographed it and projected it life-size on the wall of his studio. The wood was carved as individual sections, then assembled and laminated. A structure of clamps held the pieces in place during lamination.

Where To See Art in Wood

Alabama
Birmingham Museum of Art, Birmingham
Montgomery Museum of Fine Arts, Montgomery
Tuskegee Institute, Tuskegee

Alaska
Alaska State Museum, Juneau
Alaska Historical Library and Museum, Juneau
Sheldon Jackson Junior College Museum, Sitka

Arizona
Heard Museum, Phoenix
Phoenix Art Museum, Phoenix
Arizona State University, Tempe
University of Arizona Art Gallery, Tucson

Arkansas
Arkansas State University Museum, State University
Arkansas Arts Center, Little Rock

California
The University Art Gallery, Berkeley
Memorial Union Art Gallery,
    University of California, Davis
La Jolla Museum of Art, La Jolla
Long Beach Museum of Art, Long Beach
Los Angeles County Museum of Art, Los Angeles
Southwest Museum, Los Angeles
Oakland Art Museum, Oakland
Pasadena Art Museum, Pasadena
E. B. Crocker Art Gallery, Sacramento
San Diego Fine Arts Gallery, San Diego
DeYoung Memorial Museum and California Palace of
    the Legion of Honor, San Francisco
San Francisco Museum of Art, San Francisco
Santa Barbara Museum of Art, Santa Barbara
de Saisset Art Gallery and Museum, Santa Clara

Colorado
Denver Art Museum, Denver
Colorado Springs Fine Arts Center, Colorado Springs

Connecticut
Wadsworth Atheneum, Hartford
Marine Historical Assn., Mystic
Yale University Art Gallery, New Haven
New Britain Museum of American Art, New Britain
Wesleyan University Print Collection, Middletown
Larry Aldrich Museum, Ridgefield

Delaware
Delaware State Museum, Dover
University of Delaware Art Gallery, Newark
Delaware Art Museum, Wilmington
The Henry Francis DuPont Winterthur Museum,
    Winterthur

District of Columbia
Corcoran Gallery of Art
Freer Gallery of Art
Phillips Collection
National Collection of Fine Arts
National Gallery of Art

Florida

Lowe Art Gallery, Coral Gables
Ft. Lauderdale Museum of the Arts, Ft. Lauderdale
Cummer Gallery of Art, Jacksonville
Miami Art Center, Miami
Museum of Fine Arts, St. Petersburg
John and Mable Ringling Museum of Art, Sarasota
Norton Gallery, West Palm Beach

Georgia

Georgia Museum of Art, University of Georgia,
    Athens
High Museum of Art, Atlanta
Columbus Museum of Arts and Crafts, Columbus
Telfair Academy of Arts and Sciences, Savannah

Hawaii

Honolulu Academy of Arts, Honolulu

Idaho

Boise Art Gallery, Boise

Illinois

Krannert Art Museum, Univ. of Illinois, Champaign
The Art Institute of Chicago, Chicago
Chicago State Museum of Natural History and
    Art, Springfield

Indiana

Indiana University Department of Fine Arts,
    Bloomington
Herron Museum of Art, Indianapolis
Ft. Wayne Art Institute, Ft. Wayne
Ball State University Art Gallery, Muncie
University of Notre Dame Art Gallery, Notre Dame

Iowa

Davenport Municipal Art Gallery, Davenport
Des Moines Art Center, Des Moines

Kansas

Museum of Art, University of Kansas, Lawrence
Wichita Art Museum, Wichita

Kentucky

J. B. Speed Art Museum, Louisville

Louisiana

Isaac Delgado Museum, New Orleans
Louisiana State Museum, New Orleans

Maine

Bowdoin College Museum of Art, Brunswick
Museum of Art, Ogunquit
Portland Museum of Art, Portland
Colby College Art Museum, Waterville

Maryland

The Baltimore Museum of Art, Baltimore
Walters Art Gallery, Baltimore

Massachusetts

Phillips Academy, Andover
Fogg Art Museum, Cambridge
Boston Athenaeum, Boston
Museum of Fine Arts, Boston
Smith College Museum of Art, Northampton
Old Sturbridge Village, Old Sturbridge
Peabody Museum, Salem
Mount Holyoke College, South Hadley
Jewett Art Center, Wellesley College, Wellesley
Sterling and Francine Clark Art Institute,
    Williamstown
Worcester Art Museum, Worcester

Michigan

Museum of Art, University of Michigan, Ann Arbor
Detroit Institute of Arts, Detroit
Kresge Art Center, Michigan State University,
    East Lansing
Flint Institute of Arts, Flint
Hackley Art Gallery, Muskegon

Minnesota
Tweed Gallery, University of Minnesota, Duluth
Walker Art Center, Minneapolis
Minneapolis Institute of Arts, Minneapolis
Minnesota Historical Society, St. Paul

Mississippi
Mississippi State Historical Museum, Jackson

Missouri
William Rockhill Nelson Gallery, Kansas City
Springfield Art Museum, Springfield
Albrecht Gallery — Museum of Art, St. Joseph
City Art Museum, St. Louis

Montana
Montana Historical Society, Helena

Nebraska
Sheldon Memorial Art Gallery, University of
    Nebraska, Lincoln
Joslyn Art Museum, Omaha

Nevada
Nevada Art Gallery, Reno

New Hampshire
Saint Gaudens Museum, Cornish
Hopkins Center Art Gallery, Dartmouth College,
    Hanover
Currier Gallery of Art, Manchester

New Jersey
Monmouth County Historical Association, Freehold
Montclair Art Museum, Montclair
Newark Museum, Newark
Princeton University Art Museum, Princeton

New Mexico
University Art Gallery, Albuquerque
Roswell Museum and Art Center, Roswell
Museum of New Mexico, Santa Fe

New York
Albany Institute of History and Art, Albany
Albright-Knox Gallery, Buffalo
Arnot Art Gallery, Elmira
Museum of Art, Ithaca
Munson-Williams-Proctor, Utica
Memorial Art Gallery of the University, Rochester

New York City
Brooklyn Museum
Frick Collection
Morgan Library
Museum of Modern Art
Museum of the City of New York
Museum of the American Indian
Museum of Primitive Art
New York Public Library
Metropolitan Museum of Art
Guggenheim Museum
Whitney Museum of American Art
American Craftsmen's Council

North Carolina
Mint Museum of Art, Charlotte
Weatherspoon Art Gallery,
    University of N.C., Greensboro
William Hayes Ackland Memorial Center,
    Univ. of N.C., Chapel Hill
North Carolina Museum of Art, Raleigh
Reynolds House, Winston Salem

Ohio
Akron Art Institute, Akron
Cincinnati Art Museum, Cincinnati
Cleveland Museum of Art, Cleveland
Columbus Gallery of Fine Arts, Columbus
Dayton Art Institute, Dayton
Allen Memorial Art Museum, Oberlin College, Oberlin
Toledo Museum of Art, Toledo
Butler Institute of American Art, Youngstown
Art Institute of Zanesville, Zanesville

Oklahoma

Woolaroc Museum, Bartlesville
Oklahoma Art Center, Oklahoma City
Thomas Gilcrease Institute, Tulsa
Cowboy Hall of Fame and Western Heritage Center,
Oklahoma City

Oregon

Museum of Art, University of Oregon, Eugene
Portland Art Museum, Portland

Pennsylvania

Allentown Art Museum, Allentown
Lehigh University, Bethlehem
Bucks County Historical Society, Doylestown
Museum of Art, Carnegie Institute, Pittsburgh
Pennsylvania Academy of Fine Arts, Philadelphia
Philadelphia Museum of Art, Philadelphia
The University Museum, Univ. of Pennsylvania,
Philadelphia
Everhart Museum, Scranton

Rhode Island

Museum of Art, Rhode Island School of Design,
Providence
Newport Historical Society, Newport

South Carolina

Gibbs Art Gallery, Charleston
Columbia Museum of Art, Columbia
Bob Jones University Museum, Greenville

South Dakota

Dakota Museum, University of South Dakota,
Vermillion

Tennessee

Brooks Memorial Art Gallery, Memphis
Tennessee Fine Arts Center, Nashville

Texas

Michener Collection, University of Texas, Austin
Dallas Museum of Fine Arts, Dallas
Museum of Fine Arts, Houston
Kimball Art Foundation, Fort Worth
Fort Worth Art Center, Fort Worth
Marion Koogler McNay Art Institute, San Antonio

Utah

Harris Fine Arts Center, Brigham Young University,
Provo

Vermont

Robert Hull Fleming Museum, University of Vermont,
Burlington
Shelburne Museum, Shelburne
Bundy Art Gallery, Waitsfield

Virginia

Norfolk Museum of Arts and Science, Norfolk
The Mariners' Museum, Newport News
Virginia Museum of Fine Arts, Richmond
Colonial Williamsburg, Williamsburg

Washington

Charles and Emma Frye Museum, Seattle
Seattle Art Museum, Seattle

West Virgiina

Huntington Galleries, Huntington

Wisconsin

Elvehjem Art Center, University of Wisconsin,
Madison
Milwaukee Art Center, Milwaukee

Wyoming

Whitney Gallery of Western Art, Cody

Where to Buy Tools

Some of the tools you will require are regular carpentry items which can be purchased at your local hardware store. For carving and sculpture tools, try the nearest art supply house. Below are the names and addresses of a few firms who will send you catalogues of woodworking tools and supplies.

Sculpture Services, Inc., 9 East 19th Street, New York, N.Y. 10003

Stanley Tools, Division of The Stanley Works, New Britain, Conn. 06050

Brookstone Co., Brookstone Bldg., Peterborough, N.H. 03458

Albert Constantine and Sons, Inc., 2050 Eastchester Rd., Bronx, N.Y. 10461

Sculpture Associates, 114 East 25th Street, New York, N.Y. 10010

Craftsmans Wood Service Co., 2727 So. Mary St., Chicago, Ill. 60608

Arthur Brown & Bro., Inc., 2 West 46th Street, New York, N.Y. 10036

Woodworkers Tool Works, 222-224 S. Jefferson St., Chicago, Ill. 60606

Nasco House of Crafts, 1271 Gillingham Road, Neenah, Wisc. 54956

Minnesota Woodworkers Supply Co., 925 Winnetka North, Minneapolis, Minn. 55427

Woodcraft Supply Co., 318 Montvale Avenue, Woburn, Mass. 01801

Bibliography

The following books are not devoted exclusively to artistry in wood, but they offer interesting reading on the place of wood in the fine arts.

Art Through the Ages, by Helen Gardner. Harcourt Brace and Company. Various editions

Concise History of Modern Sculpture, by Herbert Read. Praeger. 1965

What is Modern Sculpture? by Robert Goldwater. The Museum of Modern Art, New York. 1969

Early American Wood Carving, by E. O. Christiansen. World Publishing Company. 1952

Cubism and Abstract Art, by Alfred H. Barr, Jr. The Museum of Modern Art, New York. 1936

The New Sculpture: Environments and Assemblages, by Udo Kulterman. Praeger. 1969

Constructivism: Origins and Evolution, by George Rickey. George Braziller. 1967

Beyond Modern Sculpture: The Effects of Science and Technology on the Sculpture of this Century. George Braziller 1968

Sculpture, 19th and 20th Centuries, by Fred Licht. New York Graphic Society. 1967

Evolution of Modern Sculpture, by A. M. Hammacher. Harry N. Abrams. 1969